Is Sam Sad?

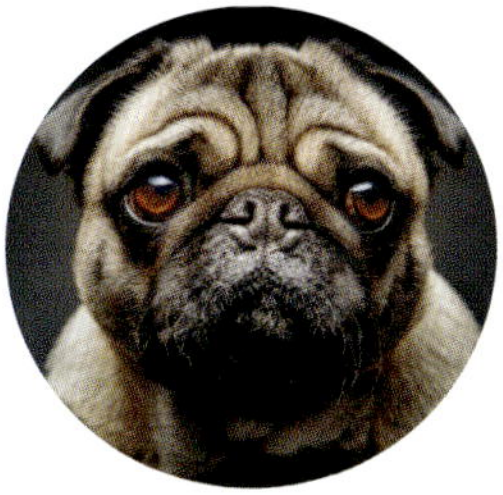

Written by
Stephen Rickard

Ransom

Is Sam sad?

Is Sam as sad as Dan?

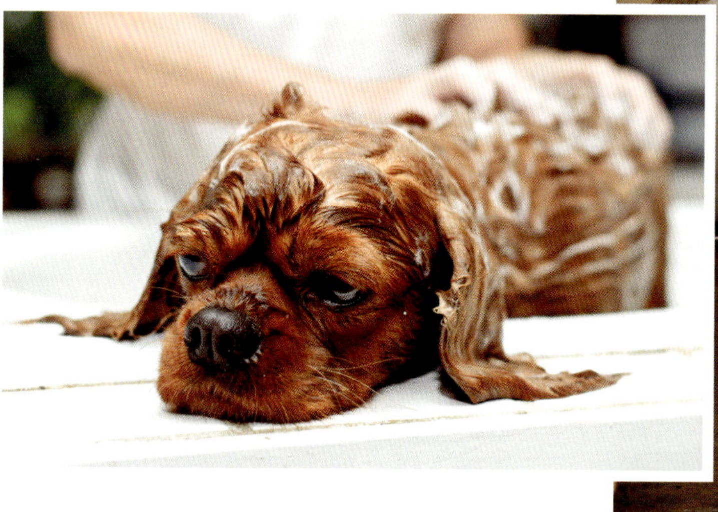

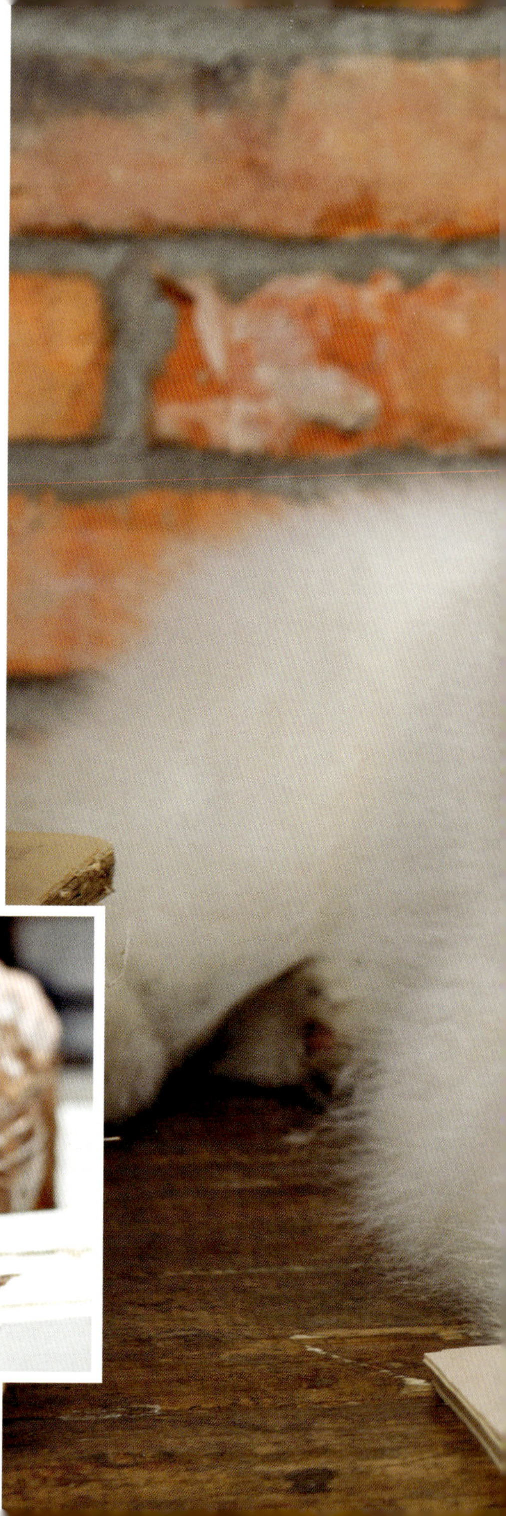

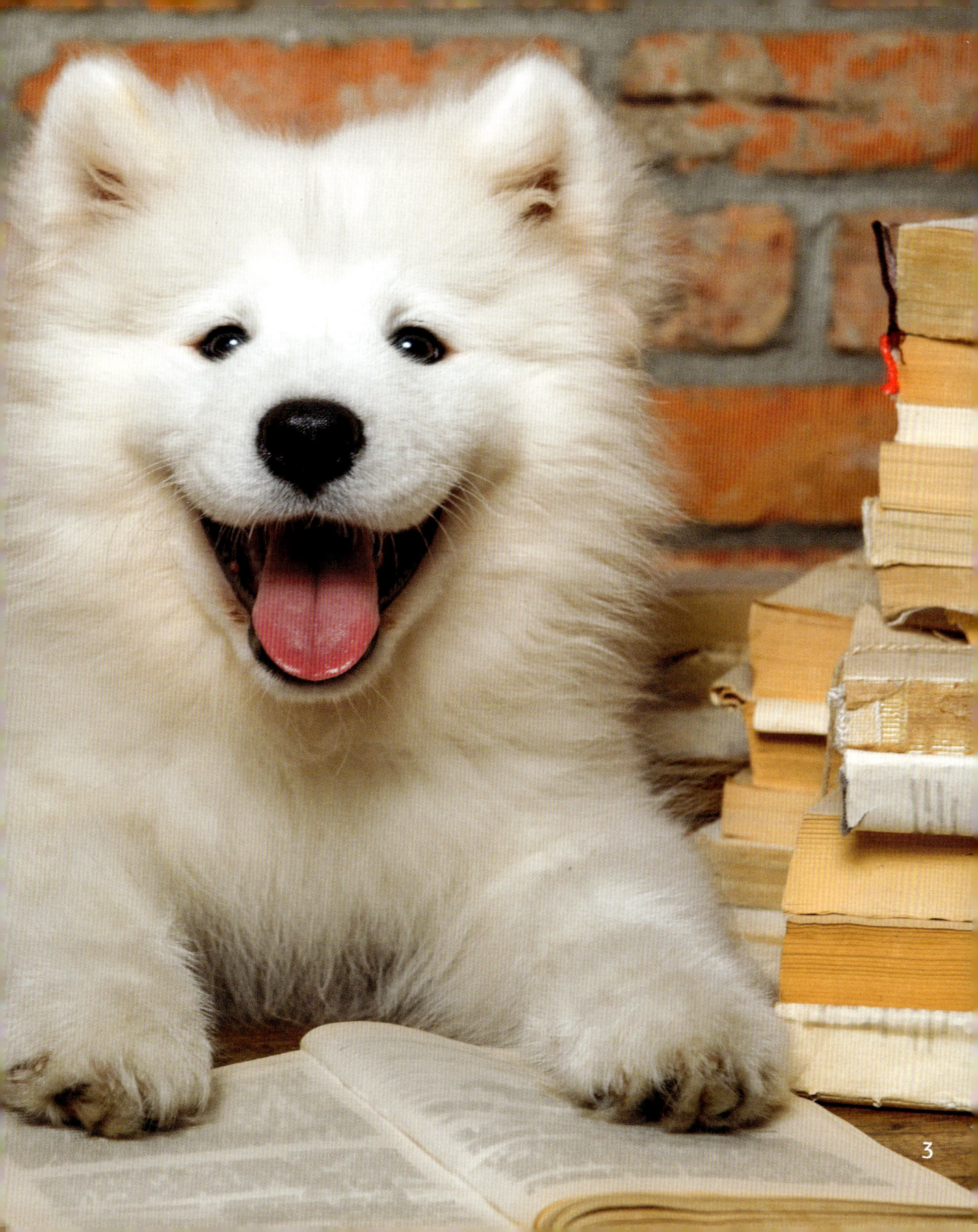

Is Tim sad?

Is Tim as sad as Pam?

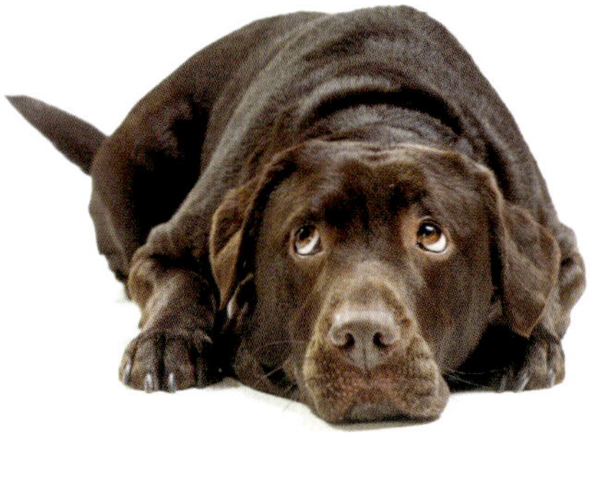

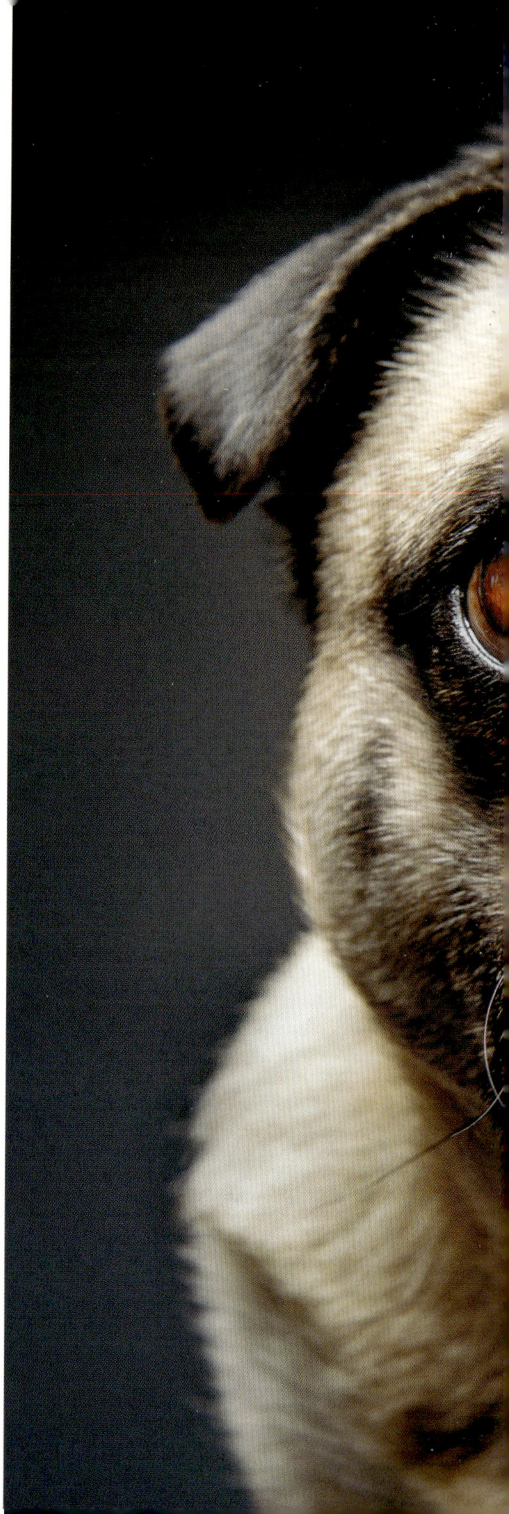

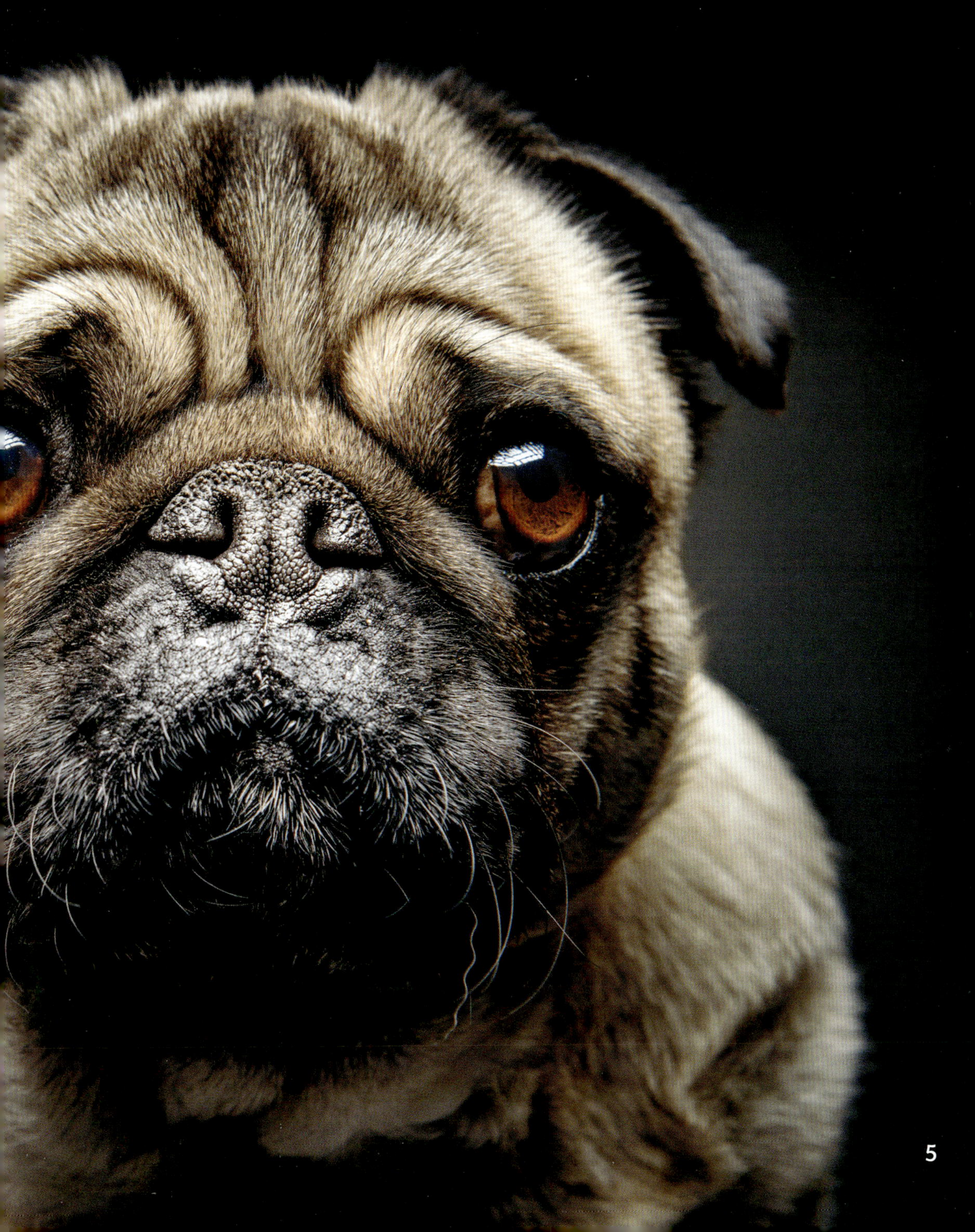

Is Pip sad?

Is Pip as sad
as Sid?

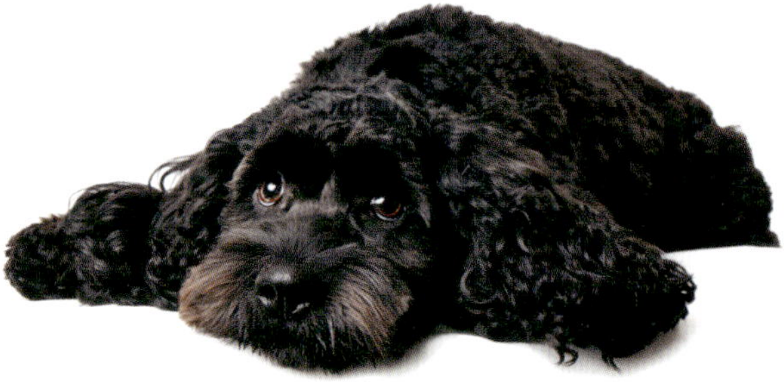

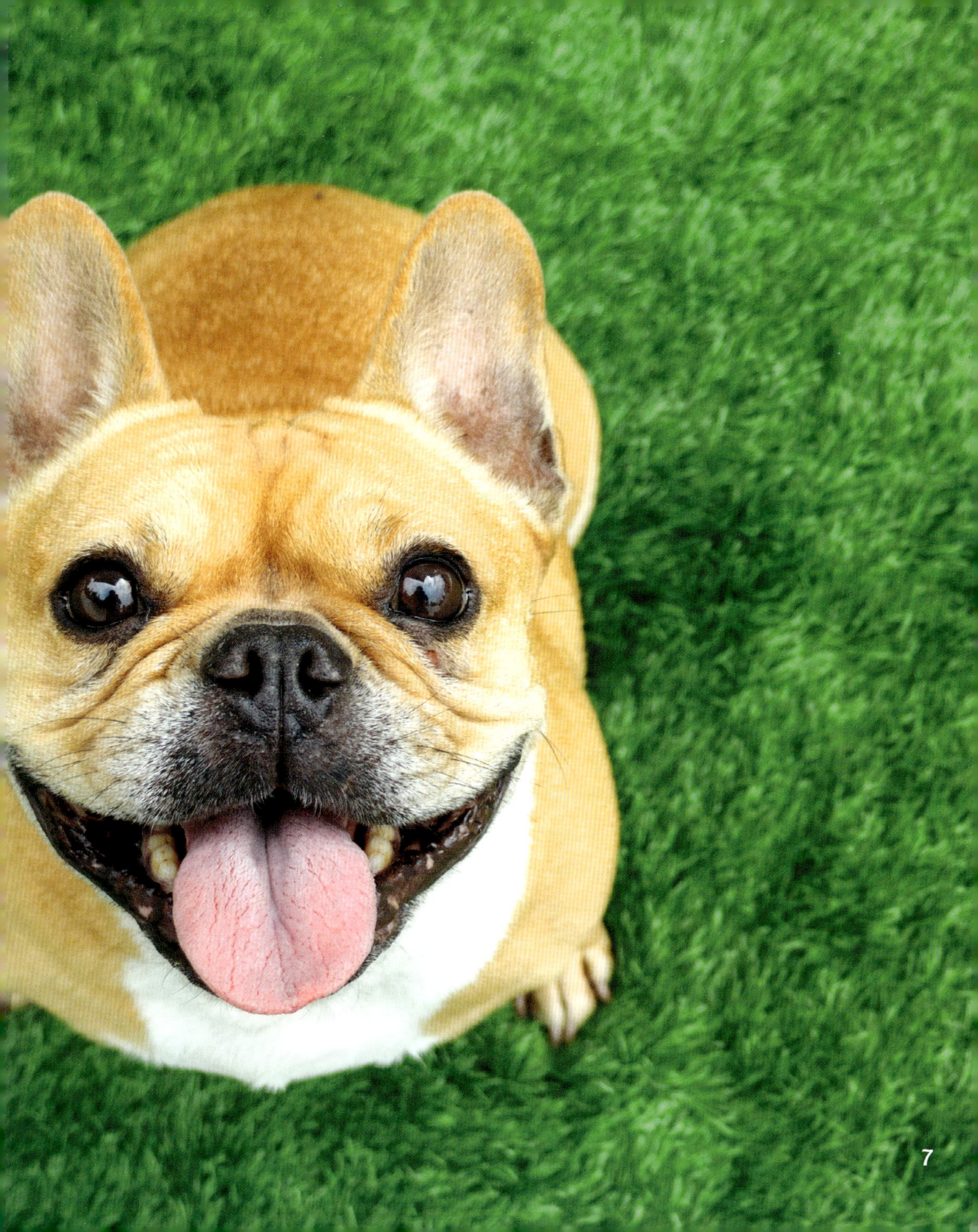

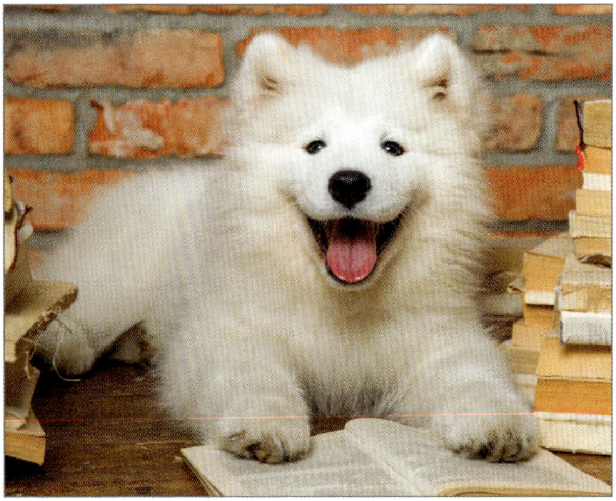

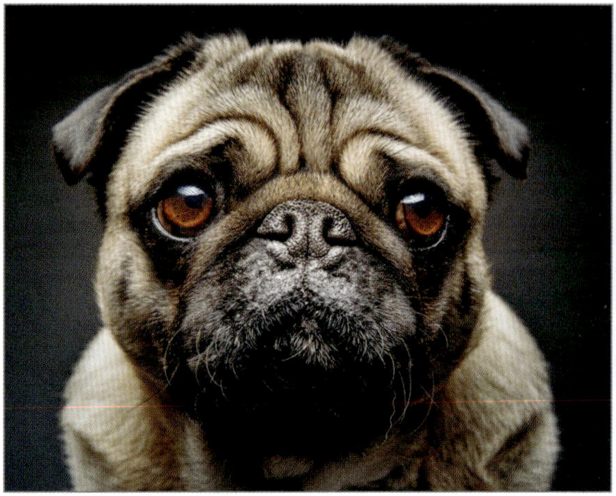

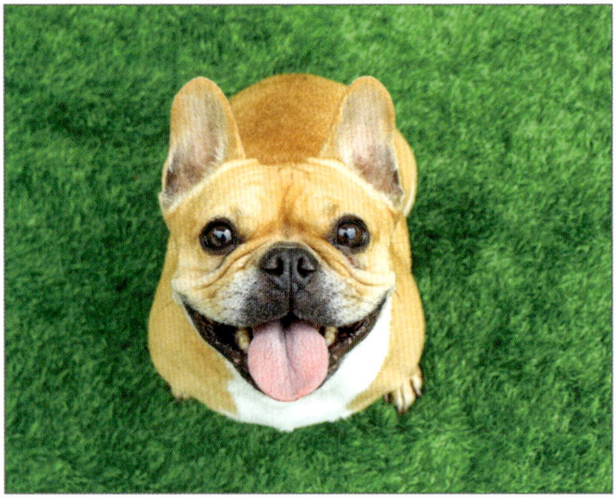

Is Sam sad?

Is Tim sad?

Is Pip sad?